CHAPTER 1

NERVOUS EMPIRES

In the late 1800s, industrial nations in Europe were looking for more **natural resources** and **markets** to expand their economies. These growing nations competed to control Africa and Asia -- a fight that we now call **imperialism**. And as the competition heated up around the globe, it increased the arguments back in Europe as well . . .

HOW NICE WAS LIFE IN THE EARLY 1900s?

MMM, LOVE A BEAUTIFUL DAY AT THE PARK! THIS **TURN OF THE CENTURY** PROMISES A MODERN WORLD OF COMFORT, PEACE... AND **JAZZ BANJO**!

HAW!

Huhn? WH-- AM I LATE?!

NOT IF YOU WANT TO SEE THE WRIGHT BROTHERS FLYING THEIR NEW AIRPLANE... OR THE PANAMA CANAL OPENING... OR TEDDY ROOSEVELT MAKING NATIONAL PARKS. IT'S AN **AGE OF PROGRESS**!

BROYD '10!

NOW LOOK, MARIAN — THOSE GERMANS HAVE STARTED THE FIRST SYSTEM OF PUBLIC WELFARE PAY! THEY'VE BEEN ON THE MARCH SINCE THOSE LITTLE STATES JOINED INTO ONE GERMAN NATION IN 1871...

GERMAN EMPIRE AN ECONOMIC SUCCESS

PETER, WHAT IS WRONG WITH THAT? THERE ARE MANY GERMAN FAMILIES IN AMERICA.

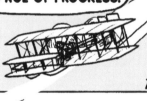

THE **SPANISH-AMERICAN WAR** IN 1898 MADE THE UNITED STATES A WORLD POWER, WITH COLONIES AND ALL.

THE U.S. NAVY'S **"GREAT WHITE FLEET"** STEAMS AROUND THE GLOBE FROM 1907 TO 1909 TO SHOW OFF. WONDER WHO IS WATCHING...

next: Scouting for **Trouble**

WHEN DID THE BOY SCOUTS START?

"SOMETHING HIDDEN. **GO** AND FIND IT! GO AND LOOK BEYOND THE RANGES— SOMETHING LOST BEHIND THE RANGES, LOST AND WAITING FOR YOU, **GO!**"

WHA-**HUH?!** IS HE DOING POETRY UNDER FIRE?!!

THAT'S HOW THE BRITISH EMPIRE ROLLS.

ROBERT BADEN -POWELL IS A GENERAL IN THIS 1902 WAR WITH SETTLERS IN SOUTH AFRICA.

BRITAIN WINS THE **BOER WAR.** BADEN-POWELL IS FAMOUS.

THE SUN NEVER SETS ON THE BRITISH EMPIRE! AND WE MUST TRAIN OUR BOYS TO BE STRONG AND SKILLED, TO KEEP THE EMPIRE GOING.

IN 1907 HE INVITES BOYS TO BROWNSEA ISLAND NEAR ENGLAND TO LEARN OUTDOOR AND SURVIVAL SKILLS.

PART II FORTNIGHTLY   PRICE 4d net
SCOUTING FOR BOYS BY **B-P**
LIEUT. GEN. BADEN POWELL

IN 1908 HE PUTS HIS IDEAS IN A BOOK. IT WILL SELL 150 MILLION COPIES IN THE 20TH CENTURY!

SO **THAT'S** A SHEEPSHANK.

PATROL! MOVE OUT!

EVERY BOY LOVES TO EXPLORE CAVES, CLIMB HILLS, **SPY** OUT STRANGE TERRITORY.

AND WE'LL NEED SPIES IN A WAR WITH GERMANY...

THE NATIONAL COMPETITION GOES ON IN OTHER AREAS...

BUILD FASTER! OUR KAISERLICHE MARINE WILL RIVAL THE FAMOUS BRITISH NAVY!

FROM 1908 TO 1913, MILITARY SPENDING BY EUROPEAN POWERS INCREASES **50 PERCENT!!**

next: KICK THE BALKAN

WHO WERE THE SERBS IN SOUTHERN EUROPE?

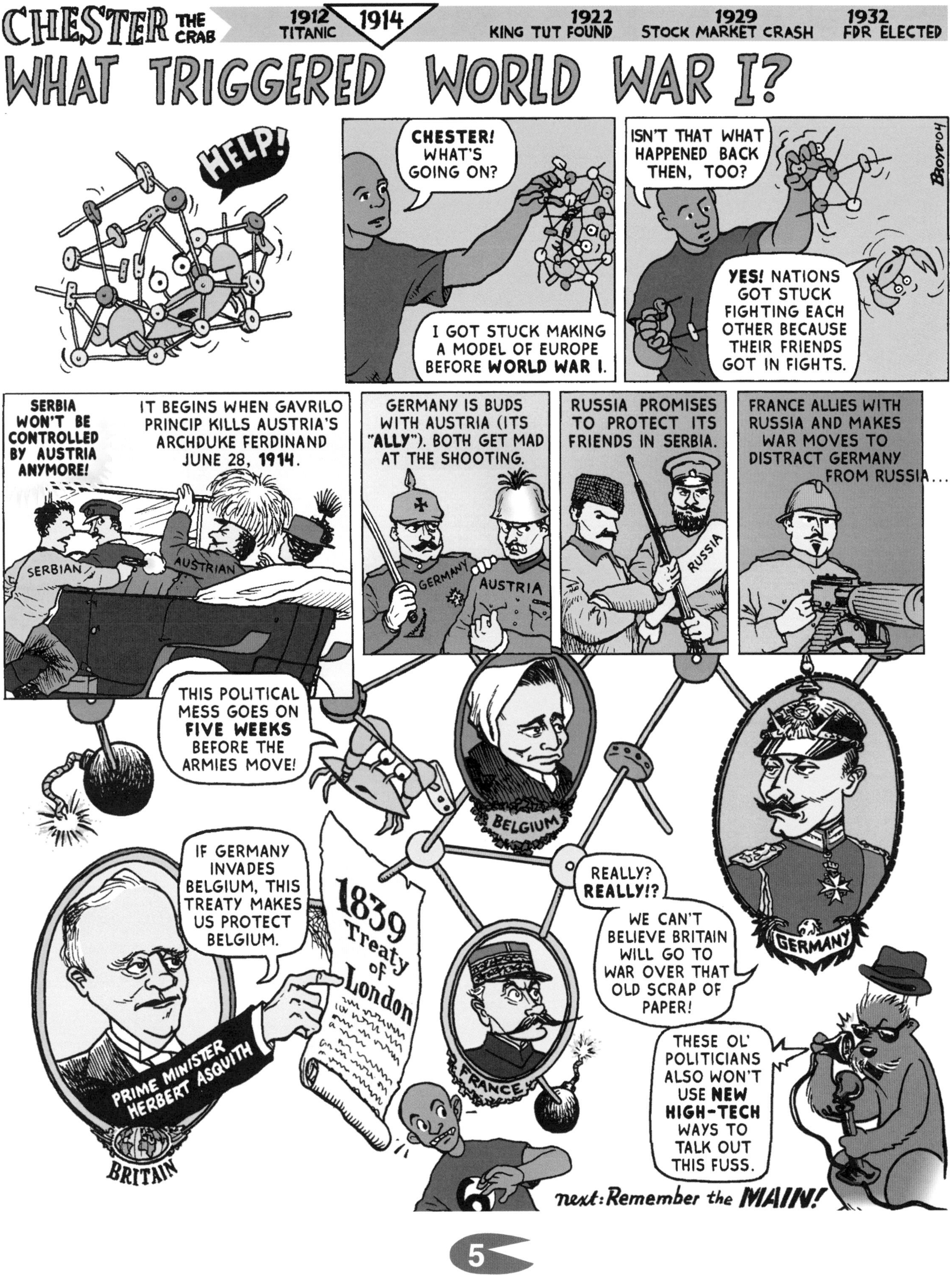

CHESTER THE CRAB
1912 TITANIC
1914
1922 KING TUT FOUND
1929 STOCK MARKET CRASH
1932 FDR ELECTED
WHAT TRIGGERED WORLD WAR I?
HELP!
CHESTER! WHAT'S GOING ON?
I GOT STUCK MAKING A MODEL OF EUROPE BEFORE WORLD WAR I.
ISN'T THAT WHAT HAPPENED BACK THEN, TOO?
YES! NATIONS GOT STUCK FIGHTING EACH OTHER BECAUSE THEIR FRIENDS GOT IN FIGHTS.
BOYD'04
SERBIA WON'T BE CONTROLLED BY AUSTRIA ANYMORE!
IT BEGINS WHEN GAVRILO PRINCIP KILLS AUSTRIA'S ARCHDUKE FERDINAND JUNE 28, 1914.
SERBIAN
AUSTRIAN
GERMANY IS BUDS WITH AUSTRIA (ITS "ALLY"). BOTH GET MAD AT THE SHOOTING.
GERMANY
AUSTRIA
RUSSIA PROMISES TO PROTECT ITS FRIENDS IN SERBIA.
RUSSIA
FRANCE ALLIES WITH RUSSIA AND MAKES WAR MOVES TO DISTRACT GERMANY FROM RUSSIA...
THIS POLITICAL MESS GOES ON FIVE WEEKS BEFORE THE ARMIES MOVE!
BELGIUM
GERMANY
IF GERMANY INVADES BELGIUM, THIS TREATY MAKES US PROTECT BELGIUM.
1839 Treaty of London
REALLY? REALLY!?
WE CAN'T BELIEVE BRITAIN WILL GO TO WAR OVER THAT OLD SCRAP OF PAPER!
PRIME MINISTER HERBERT ASQUITH
BRITAIN
FRANCE
THESE OL' POLITICIANS ALSO WON'T USE NEW HIGH-TECH WAYS TO TALK OUT THIS FUSS.
next: Remember the MAIN!

WHY DID SERB STRAINS LEAD TO A BIG WAR?

THERE HAD BEEN A LOT OF SKIRMISHES IN THE 20 YEARS BEFORE WORLD WAR I – EVEN THE SPANISH-AMERICAN WAR WAS QUICK. SO **WHY** DOES **THIS** WAR GET SO BIG?!?

MUNITIONS

SPENDING ON MILITARY STUFF **TRIPLES** IN BRITAIN AND GERMANY FROM 1875 TO 1914. THERE ARE NOW **19 MILLION MEN** ON ACTIVE DUTY OR RESERVE IN EUROPE'S ARMIES.

ALLIES

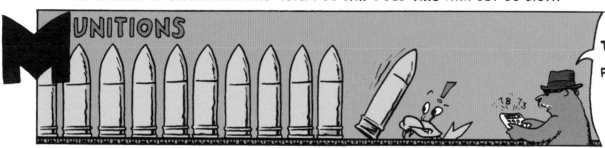

FRANCE · BRITAIN · ITALY · RUSSIA

THE BRITISH WILL FIGHT ON EUROPEAN SOIL FOR THE **FIRST** TIME SINCE BEATING NAPOLEON IN THE BATTLE OF WATERLOO IN 1815!

IMPERIALISM

BRITAIN THINKS IT CAN WIN BECAUSE OF ITS EMPIRE — IT WILL RECRUIT **8.6 MILLION** MEN WORLDWIDE INTO THIS WAR. AND THE WINNERS HOPE TO TAKE THE LOSER'S COLONIES.

NATIONALISM

OUR FLAG IS BETTER THAN THEIR FLAG!

PEOPLE TEND TO CLING TO THEIR FAMILY OR TOWN. BUT THE RISIN' POWER OF MODERN NATIONS DRAWS FOLKS INTO THIS LARGER GROUPING... A POWERFUL PULL OF **PATRIOTISM**.

THE LAMPS ARE GOING OUT ALL OVER EUROPE. WE SHALL NOT SEE THEM LIT AGAIN IN OUR LIFETIME...

KEY: ALLIES
CENTRAL POWERS
NEUTRAL

IRELAND · BRITAIN · LONDON · BELGIUM · HOLLAND · PARIS · BERLIN · GERMANY · SWITZERLAND · FRANCE · ITALY · ROME · AUSTRIA-HUNGARY · ROMANIA · SERBIA · BULGARIA · MONTENEGRO · ALBANIA · GREECE · RUSSIA · TURKEY

N W E S

OUR LEADERS SAY IT WILL BE QUICK VICTORY — LIKE OUR WIN AT SEDAN IN 1870. BUT WEAPONS HAVE **CHANGED**. GOING ON OFFENSE WILL BE MUCH HARDER THAN PLAYING DEFENSE!

NO MAN'S LAND

After the surge of **nationalistic feelings** and **militarism** caused diplomacy to fail, the arguments between allies carried to the battlefield. Leaders and patriots in each nation were sure that their army (and their friends in the allied army) would quickly carry the day. But the changes in weapons and transportation in the years right before the **"Great War"** meant big surprises for the leaders and big tragedies for the fighting men.

WHY DID THE 1ST BATTLES BOG DOWN?

CHESTER THE CRAB

1912 TITANIC | 1916 | 1922 KING TUT FOUND | 1929 STOCK MARKET CRASH | 1932 FDR ELECTED

WHAT HAPPENS IN THE MUD AT VERDUN?

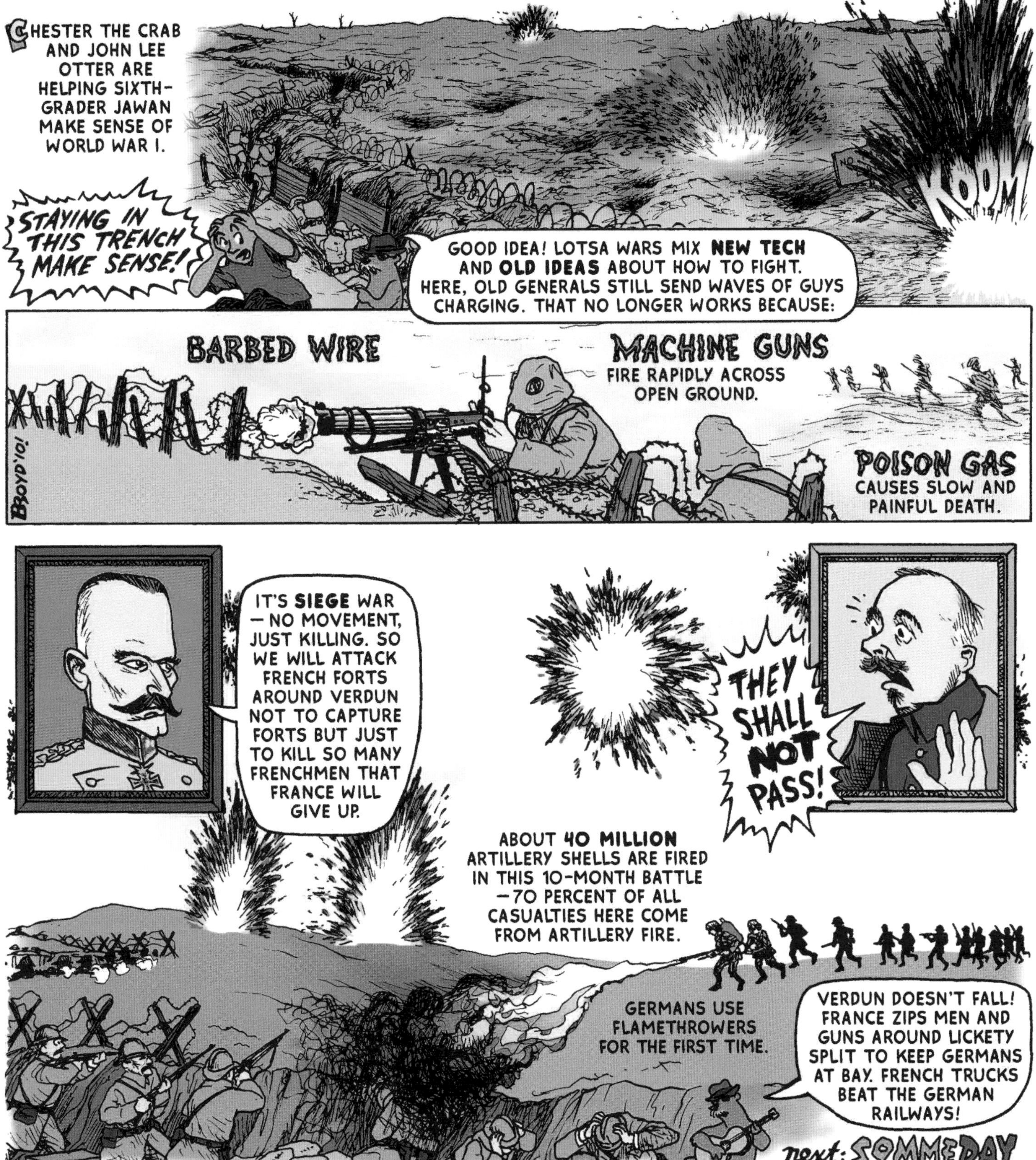
CHESTER THE CRAB AND JOHN LEE OTTER ARE HELPING SIXTH-GRADER JAWAN MAKE SENSE OF WORLD WAR I.
STAYING IN THIS TRENCH MAKE SENSE!
GOOD IDEA! LOTSA WARS MIX NEW TECH AND OLD IDEAS ABOUT HOW TO FIGHT. HERE, OLD GENERALS STILL SEND WAVES OF GUYS CHARGING. THAT NO LONGER WORKS BECAUSE:
BARBED WIRE
MACHINE GUNS
FIRE RAPIDLY ACROSS OPEN GROUND.
POISON GAS
CAUSES SLOW AND PAINFUL DEATH.
BBOYD'10!
IT'S SIEGE WAR — NO MOVEMENT, JUST KILLING. SO WE WILL ATTACK FRENCH FORTS AROUND VERDUN NOT TO CAPTURE FORTS BUT JUST TO KILL SO MANY FRENCHMEN THAT FRANCE WILL GIVE UP.
THEY SHALL NOT PASS!
ABOUT 40 MILLION ARTILLERY SHELLS ARE FIRED IN THIS 10-MONTH BATTLE —70 PERCENT OF ALL CASUALTIES HERE COME FROM ARTILLERY FIRE.
GERMANS USE FLAMETHROWERS FOR THE FIRST TIME.
VERDUN DOESN'T FALL! FRANCE ZIPS MEN AND GUNS AROUND LICKETY SPLIT TO KEEP GERMANS AT BAY. FRENCH TRUCKS BEAT THE GERMAN RAILWAYS!
next: SOMMEDAY

WHAT WAS WRONG IN THE BATTLE OF THE SOMME?

ARTILLERY IS MUCH BIGGER AND BADDER IN THIS WAR. IN JUST ONE WEEK IN JUNE 1916, THE BRITISH FIRE **1.7 MILLION** SHELLS AT GERMAN TRENCHES NEAR THE **SOMME RIVER!**

BOOM

KEEP FIRING!! FIGHTING "JERRY" HERE TAKES PRESSURE OFF FRENCH SOLDIERS AT VERDUN!

BUT GERMAN TROOPS SIT IN DEEP BUNKERS, UNHURT.

THE BRITS MAKE NOISE, BUT THEIR GUNS CAN'T REACH US DOWN HERE.

THE BRITISH LIFT THE BOMBARDMENT TO ATTACK ACROSS NO-MAN'S LAND. BUT GERMANS RUSH UP FROM THE BUNKERS AND TO THEIR MACHINE GUNS...

BUDDABUDDABU BUDM

AAAH!

BOYD '10!

IT'S ONLY A MILE TO THE GERMAN LINES! LET'S GAHK AKH!

THIS FIRST WAVE OF THE SOMME ATTACK MAKES 57,470 BRITISH DEAD, WOUNDED, OR MISSING. JULY 1, 1916, IS THE BLOODIEST DAY IN THE HISTORY OF THE BRITISH ARMY.

KLIK!

THE SOMME FIGHT GRINDS ON FIVE MONTHS. IN SEPTEMBER **TANKS** ARE USED FOR THE FIRST TIME — BUT AT 2 MPH. BY NOVEMBER THE BRITS HAVE LOST 420,000 MEN TO GAIN JUST **TWO MILES OF LAND!**

AHRR! WE GO ON KILLING FOR NO REASON. THIS IS A WAR AGAINST RELIGION AND CIVILIZATION...

next: *Plane Crazy*

HOW DID AIRPLANES JOIN WARFARE?

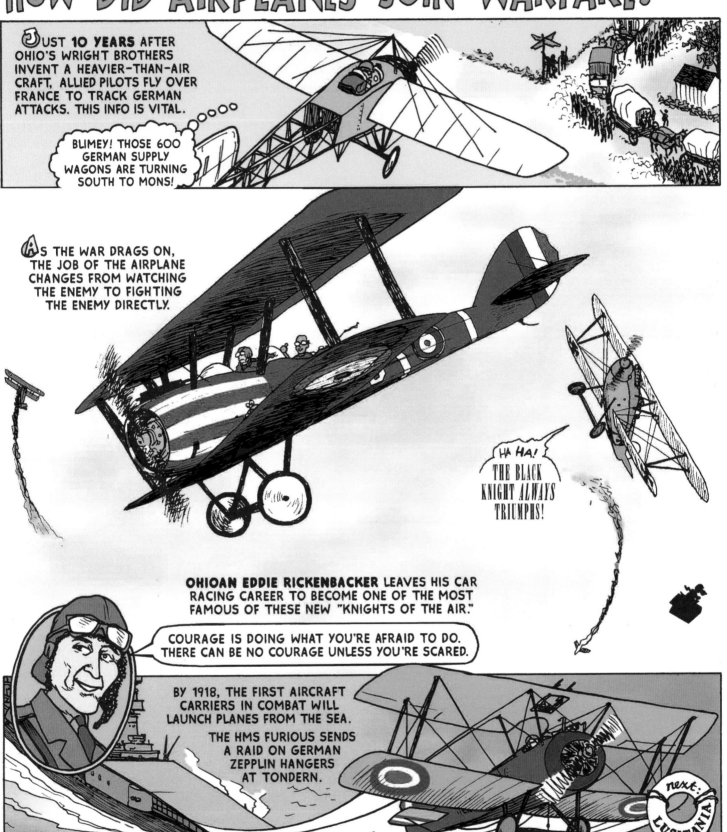

Just **10 YEARS** AFTER OHIO'S WRIGHT BROTHERS INVENT A HEAVIER-THAN-AIR CRAFT, ALLIED PILOTS FLY OVER FRANCE TO TRACK GERMAN ATTACKS. THIS INFO IS VITAL.

BLIMEY! THOSE 600 GERMAN SUPPLY WAGONS ARE TURNING SOUTH TO MONS!

As THE WAR DRAGS ON, THE JOB OF THE AIRPLANE CHANGES FROM WATCHING THE ENEMY TO FIGHTING THE ENEMY DIRECTLY.

HA HA! THE BLACK KNIGHT *ALWAYS* TRIUMPHS!

OHIOAN EDDIE RICKENBACKER LEAVES HIS CAR RACING CAREER TO BECOME ONE OF THE MOST FAMOUS OF THESE NEW "KNIGHTS OF THE AIR."

COURAGE IS DOING WHAT YOU'RE AFRAID TO DO. THERE CAN BE NO COURAGE UNLESS YOU'RE SCARED.

BY 1918, THE FIRST AIRCRAFT CARRIERS IN COMBAT WILL LAUNCH PLANES FROM THE SEA.

THE HMS FURIOUS SENDS A RAID ON GERMAN ZEPPLIN HANGERS AT TONDERN.

next: LUSITANIA

WHY DID THE LUSITANIA NOT DRAG THE U.S. TO WAR?

BRITAIN'S NAVY **BLOCKADES** GERMAN PORTS TO CUT OFF MILITARY SUPPLIES TO THEM. BRITAIN EVEN MINES BIG SECTIONS OF SEA LANES.

BOWZERS! THAT PUTS EVEN TALKING ANIMALS IN DANGER!

SORRY, CHAPS, THIS IS NOW **TOTAL WAR!**

OUR GERMAN LEADERS DECLARE A WAR ZONE AROUND BRITAIN. WE ARE ORDERED TO SINK **ALL** SHIPS TAKING SUPPLIES TO BRITAIN!

BKOOM

THIS IS THE FIRST WAR WHERE SUBMARINES CAUSE A LOT OF DAMAGE AND DEATH.

BBOYD '04

ON MAY 7, **1915**, GERMANS SINK THE PASSENGER SHIP **LUSITANIA**.

WE'RE **NOT** A BATTLESHIP!

THIS SHIP CARRIES AMMUNITION FOR THE WAR. BUT 1,200 PEOPLE DIE IN THE SINKING — INCLUDING 128 AMERICANS. ARE AMERICANS MAD ENOUGH TO JOIN THE FIGHT **NOW**?

NO! UNITED STATES PRESIDENT **WOODROW WILSON** KEEPS AMERICA OUT.

THERE IS SUCH A THING AS A NATION BEING SO RIGHT IT DOES NOT NEED TO CONVINCE OTHERS BY FORCE.

THIS FITS WITH AMERICA'S LONG TRADITION OF STAYING OUT OF EUROPE'S BATTLES.

JOPLIN: RAGTIME MUSIC HERE TO STAY

EUROPE WAR RAGES

WE'RE **NEUTRAL!** WE ARE NOT PICKING SIDES.

BESIDES, THE U.S. HAS PROBLEMS CLOSER TO HOME —

PANCHO VILLA WILL BOOT YANKEES!!

AMERICA OVER THERE

Every bloody, terrible month that the war continued made it harder for the United States to remain **neutral**. The U.S. had a **long tradition of avoiding involvement in European conflicts**, but that tradition was clashing more and more with **America's business interests** and **growth into a global superpower** after the Spanish-American War. After waiting out the war for years, it won't take much in 1917 to bring the U.S. into the fight . . .

WHY DID AMERICA JOIN WORLD WAR I?

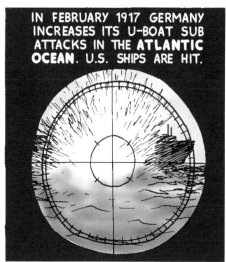

HOW DID AMERICA PREPARE FOR WAR?

AT THE START OF WORLD WAR I, MOST OF AMERICA'S EXPERIENCED SOLDIERS ARE IN THE **MARINES**. WHEN THE U.S. JOINS THE WAR, IT HAS 13,725 OFFICERS AND SOLDIERS IN THE MARINE CORPS — IN ANOTHER YEAR THE MARINES WILL HAVE **75,101 MEN!**

YOU GOTTA PUT ALL THOSE GUYS SOMEPLACE. SO THE MARINE CORPS BUILDS A BASE IN **QUANTICO**, VIRGINIA, IN MAY 1917.

BLOYD '10!

WE WILL BE ON THIS FIRING RANGE UNTIL YOU CAN HIT A HUN AT **800 YARDS!**

BUT THE BUILDUP TAKES TIME. WE DON'T EVEN HAVE ENOUGH SHIPS TO GET MEN TO THE BATTLEFIELDS. **HALF** THE U.S. TROOPS WHO CROSS THE ATLANTIC DO SO IN BRITISH SHIPS!

MEANWHILE, TIRED FRENCH TROOPS MUTINY AND SING SOCIALIST SONGS AGAINST THEIR GOVERNMENT.

GENERAL **JOHN "BLACK JACK" PERSHING** LEADS AMERICAN TROOPS IN EUROPE. HE REMINDS FRANCE IT ONCE SENT SOLDIERS AND A YOUNG, DASHING LEADER TO HELP WIN **OUR** REVOLUTION. NOW AMERICA RETURNS THE FAVOR!

LAFAYETTE, WE ARE HERE!

Quelle blague! THE AMERICANS HAVE NOT BEEN SEASONED IN A REAL FIGHT. THEY ARE LIKE UNBAKED BREAD.

THEY ARE "*DOUGHBOYS!*"

next: HOME FREEZE

WHAT FREEDOMS VANISHED ON THE HOMEFRONT?

DON'T KNOW, GUYS... AFTER ALL THE KILLING IN THE WAR, HOW COULD AMERICANS GET EXCITED ABOUT

STOP! STOP RIGHT THERE! NO MORE OF **THAT** KIND OF TALK!

WAKE UP, AMERICA!
CIVILIZATION CALLS EVERY MAN WOMAN AND CHILD!

HUH? CAN'T I

NO YOU CAN'T! CONGRESS PASSED THE **SEDITION ACT!** YOU CAN GO TO JAIL **20 YEARS** FOR SAYING OR WRITING ANYTHING DISLOYAL TO THE GOVERNMENT OF THE UNITED STATES.

NOW **THAT'S** CENSORSHIP!

PRESIDENT WOODROW WILSON ALSO PUSHES A NEW **ESPIONAGE ACT.** THE POSTAL SERVICE STOPS DELIVERING ALMOST ALL PUBLICATIONS. LIBRARIANS MUST REPORT WEIRD REQUESTS.

Over there! Over there!

Welcome to another *Liberty Sing*

WE BANNED THE SONG "I WONDER WHO'S KISSING HER NOW" SO SOLDIERS WON'T WORRY!

WILSON'S TEAM USES NEW MASS ADVERTISING TRICKS...

FWLAK

THE MAIN TARGET OF NEW SUSPICION IS **GERMAN-AMERICANS.** STATES EVEN OUTLAW THE TEACHING OF GERMAN IN SCHOOLS!

WE'RE RENAMING SAUERKRAUT "LIBERTY CABBAGE!"

HMMMM. THIS REMINDS ME OF "FREEDOM FRIES."

THE U.S. JUSTICE DEPARTMENT GIVES BADGES TO 200,000 VOLUNTEERS SO THEY CAN SPY ON NEIGHBORS. THESE "SECRET SERVICE" AGENTS GO AFTER "SLACKERS" AND BULLY PEOPLE INTO BUYING LIBERTY BONDS TO PAY FOR THE WAR.

SOCIALIST!

CA-REEEEEPY!

next: **RED DAWN**

DID THE RUSSIAN REVOLUTION END THE WAR?

REMEMBER HOW THIS WAR STARTS PARTLY BECAUSE **RUSSIA** TRIES TO HELP **SERBS** IN EASTERN EUROPE? HERE'S HOW THAT WORKS OUT:

RETREAT! THE GERMANS CAN **HAVE** POLAND!

St. PETERSBURG

IN **MARCH 1917** RUSSIANS IN PETROGRAD PROTEST **CZAR NICHOLAS II** AND HIS ROMANOV FAMILY.

BREAD! LAND! PEACE!

LENIN (NOT LENNON)

CZAR NICHOLAS LEAVES POWER. CONFUSION IN THE GOVERNMENT LEADS TO CONFUSION IN THE RUSSIAN ARMY.

BOIS CARRE

BOA КАРРЭ

I MISS RUSSIAN BLACK BREAD...

WHY ARE WE FIGHTING IN THIS MESS?!

WE ARE SOLD FOR SHELLS. CANNON FODDER! WHITE SLAVES TO CAPITALISM!!

RUSSIAN SOLDIERS IN FRANCE FIGHT **EACH OTHER** - 8,000 SOCIALIST TROOPS MUTINY IN SEPTEMBER!

IT'S THE FIRST FIGHT OF THE **RUSSIAN CIVIL WAR.**

sigh

THE SOCIALIST BOLSHEVIKS TAKE CHARGE OF RUSSIA IN NOVEMBER. THEY SET A CEASE-FIRE WITH GERMANY. THE **TREATY OF BREST-LITOVSK** IN MARCH 1918 TAKES RUSSIAN SOLDIERS OUT OF WORLD WAR I.

SO WHAT WAS THE POINT OF ALL THAT??

CHAPTER 4

ARMISTICE AND AFTERMATH

This global war has killed millions, transformed European and American life, and wrecked the economies of Europe. Is there a way to bring it to a close? Is there any "victory" for anyone? Germany thinks it can still win with one last push. France and Britain want to win so they can take over the colonies of Germany and the Ottoman Empire. What role will the United States play in the end of this drama?

WHEN DID GERMANY ALMOST WIN WWI?

London
Britain
English Channel
Ypres
Belgium
SOMME R.
Amiens
France
SEINE R.
Paris
HINDENBURG LINE

ⓘN **MARCH 1918**, THE GERMAN ARMY TRIES A BIG ATTACK TO WIN THE WAR BEFORE AMERICAN TROOPS SHOW UP.

WITH RUSSIA OUT OF THE WAR, WE CAN FINALLY PUT **ALL** OUR TROOPS IN FRANCE!

GENERAL ERICH LUDENDORFF

INSTEAD OF ONE BIG WAVE OF SOLDIERS RUNNING ACROSS "NO MAN'S LAND," SMALL SQUADS OF GERMAN **STORMTROOPERS** SHOCK WEAK SPOTS AND GO AROUND BIG DEFENSES.

SEE YOU IN PARIS!

THE GERMANS GET **WITHIN 75 MILES OF PARIS!!** HEAVY KRUPP RAILWAY GUNS FIRE SHELLS INTO PARIS!

YAH!

BUT MOST GERMAN ARTILLERY IS **NOT** MOTORIZED. AND GERMANS HAVE FEW TANKS.

NEW AMERICAN SOLDIERS JUMP INTO WEAKENED FRENCH AND BRITISH UNITS TO STOP THE ADVANCE.

VIVE Le HARLEM HELLFIGHTERZ!

MEANWHILE... RICKENBACKER BLAZES THROUGH THE SKIES!

CH-CHOKA CHOKA CHOKA

THE AMERICAN SHOOTS DOWN 26 ENEMY AIRCRAFT DURING HIS 300 COMBAT HOURS — THE MOST OF ANY U.S. PILOT IN THE WAR.

next: THE WOOD

WHO WINS BELLEAU WOOD & CHATEAU-THIERRY?

AFTER YEARS OF GRINDING TRENCH WARFARE, SUDDENLY **ALL** THE ARMIES ARE ON THE MOVE IN **JUNE 1918**...

YOU AMERICAN MARINES! FALL BACK WIT' US!

RETREAT? **HELL!** WE JUST GOT HERE!

THE MARINES COUNTERATTACK GERMAN MACHINEGUN TEAMS IN THE **BELLEAU WOOD**.

IN THE FIRST DAY OF FIGHTING IN THE WOOD, THE 4TH MARINE BRIGADE TAKES **MORE** CASUALTIES THAN THE MARINE CORPS HAD TAKEN IN ITS **FIRST 142 YEARS!** IT TAKES 20 MORE DAYS OF FIGHTING BEFORE A MARINE CAN SAY:

WOODS NOW U.S. MARINE CORPS' ENTIRELY.

ON JULY 15, GERMANS PUSH WEST FROM **CHATEAU-THIERRY**. THE U.S. 2ND DIVISION RUSHES TO STOP THEM, MARCHING OVERNIGHT!

THE HUNS WON'T CROSS CHATEAU-THIERRY TODAY!!

THEY HAVE 15,000 OF US PRISONER. THE END IS NEAR...

AMERICANS ATTACK **ST. MIHIEL** ON SEPT. 12, 1918. THEY TAKE THE VILLAGE OF THIAUCOURT — CONTROLLED BY GERMANS SINCE SEPTEMBER 1914!

next: **100 Days = ?**

WHO WINS "THE 100 DAYS OFFENSIVE?"

GERMANY'S BIG PUSH IN THE SPRING OF 1918 COSTS IT 270,000 MEN KILLED AND WOUNDED. AND BY JULY ITS TROOPS HAVE BEEN PUSHED BACK TO WHERE THEY WERE IN JANUARY!

Ach!

IN GERMANY, PEOPLE ARE HUNGRY AND TIRED OF WAR.

Grwwlwll

Ratten! OUR FACTORIES ARE MAKING ONLY 53% OF WHAT THEY DID IN 1913.

10,000 AMERICAN SOLDIERS NOW ARRIVE IN FRANCE **EVERY DAY!** THESE FRESH TROOPS COMBINE WITH BRITISH AND FRENCH TANKS TO ROLL BACK THE GERMANS.

NICE SHELL!

FINALLY, WE ARE SAFE FROM MACHINE GUNS!

Huhn! **YOU** ARE!

THE ALLIED "HUNDRED DAYS OFFENSIVE" BEGINS AUGUST 8 IN **THE BATTLE OF AMIENS** — NOW CALLED "THE BLACK DAY OF THE GERMAN ARMY."

U.S. SOLDIERS PUSH THROUGH THE HILLY **ARGONNE FOREST** IN OCTOBER.

OVER THE TOP!

WE CANNOT WIN THE WAR. BUT WE MUST **NOT LOSE** IT EITHER!

LUDENDORFF ORDERS THE GERMAN NAVY TO ATTACK. SAILORS AT KIEL REFUSE.

MORE FIGHTING IS SUICIDE!

U.S. PRESIDENT **WOODROW WILSON** DEMANDS THAT GERMANY'S KAISER LEAVE POWER. ON NOVEMBER 9, OTHER GERMAN POLITICIANS TAKE OVER AND DECLARE THE NEW **WEIMAR REPUBLIC.**

TICKET TO FIGHT

ON THE 11TH HOUR OF THE 11TH DAY OF THE 11TH MONTH OF 1918, A CEASE-FIRE ("**ARMISTICE**") IS SIGNED IN A RAIL CAR IN FRANCE'S EASTERN WOODS.

next: **FLU** SHOT

HOW MANY DIED FROM THE "SPANISH FLU?"

"THE GREAT WAR" MOBILIZED 74 MILLION MEN. ABOUT **10 MILLION OF THEM DIED IN BATTLE**, AND 30 MILLION WERE WOUNDED.

BUT **DEATH STILL STALKS THE GLOBE**, MARCHING BESIDE THE SOLDIERS WHO HAVE SURVIVED THE BATTLEFIELDS...

IN JANUARY AND FEBRUARY 1918, A **POWERFUL FLU** HITS A FARMING COMMUNITY IN KANSAS.

SOLDIERS VISITING THE TOWN CARRY THE FLU BUG TO THE SECOND-LARGEST CAMP FOR NEW SOLDIERS IN THE U.S.

THESE SOLDIERS CARRY THE FLU TO EUROPE.

THE DISEASE GETS NAMED **SPANISH FLU** BECAUSE IT IS THERE WHEN PEOPLE NOTICE ITS DAMAGE.

IT IS SWIFT! IN THE FALL OF 1918 THIS FLU KILLS MORE PEOPLE IN 24 WEEKS THAN AIDS KILLS IN 24 YEARS.

SAMOA IN THE PACIFIC OCEAN LOSES 25% OF ITS POPULATION!

DEADLY DISEASE HAS BEEN A PART OF **EVERY** BIG WAR. BUT FLU IS NASTY 'CAUSE IT CAN JUMP FROM PERSON TO PERSON BEFORE EITHER SHOWS SIGNS OF BEING SICK!

SOLDIERS GOING HOME FROM THE WAR TAKE THE FLU WITH THEM. ABOUT **17 MILLION** PEOPLE IN INDIA DIE FROM THE FLU!!

MODERN SCIENTISTS SAY THE SPANISH FLU KILLS MAYBE

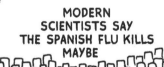

50 MILLION WORLDWIDE — MORE PEOPLE THAN **ANY OTHER DISEASE OUTBREAK** IN HUMAN HISTORY!

AND ONE VICTIM COULD BE **THE PRESIDENT**...

next: **BIG LEAGUE**

HOW DID WILSON SHAPE THE PEACE?

IN THE GREAT FLU EPIDEMIC OF 1918, MANY VICTIMS SHOW SIGNS OF DEMENTIA. THIS FLU VIRUS CAN REALLY AFFECT A PERSON'S BRAIN.

...AND THE FLU IS FLOATING THROUGH PARIS, FRANCE, WHEN UNITED STATES PRESIDENT WOODROW WILSON GOES TO MAKE PEACE BASED ON HIS "14 POINTS."

...#4: REDUCTION OF NATIONAL WEAPONS. #5: A FAIR REWORKING OF EUROPEAN COLONIES...

THANK YOU, WOODY!

FORGET THAT! WE WON! WE'LL TAKE ALL WE CAN

GERMANY / ITALY / BRITAIN / FRANCE

WILSON'S DAUGHTER GETS THE FLU IN FEBRUARY 1919 (A MONTH WHEN 2,676 PARISIANS DIE FROM THE FLU). IN MARCH HIS WIFE AND DOCTOR GET IT.

AND IN APRIL...

KOFF HACK GASP WHEEZ

WILSON'S TEMPERATURE HITS **103°** HE TRIES TO NEGOTIATE FROM HIS SICKBED, BUT HIS MIND TURNS CRANKY AND ODD.

HERE ARE YOUR FRENCH FRIES.

FRENCH SPIES?!

HE CANNOT KEEP THINGS OUT OF THE TREATY.

GERMANY PAYS FOR STARTING THE WAR — **$33 BILLION** IN **REPARATIONS** TO US!

Fine... jus'.FINE.

THIS TREATY WILL CREATE **NINE** NEW NATIONS!

IT TAKES HALF A YEAR TO HAMMER OUT THE TREATY OF VERSAILLES ("VER-SEYE"). IT IGNORES MOST OF WILSON'S 14 POINTS BUT INCLUDES HIS PLAN FOR A **LEAGUE OF NATIONS**.

NEXT TIME WE'LL TALK OUT OUR PROBLEMS, NOT GO TO WAR.

WILSON CAMPAIGNS ACROSS THE U.S. TO GET THE TREATY PASSED.

WE WILL MAINTAIN PEACE BY MAINTAINING **RIGHT** AND **JUSTICE!**

DURING THIS BRUTAL SCHEDULE, HE HAS A MAJOR STROKE IN SEPTEMBER 1919.

U.S. SENATORS WON'T LET THE U.S. JOIN THE LEAGUE **OR** SIGN THE TREATY ENDING THE WAR! STILL, THE STAGE IS SET FOR THE U.S. TO BE A WORLD POWER...

HOW DID WWI CHANGE AMERICA?

AFTER WORLD WAR I, AMERICA PULLS BACK FROM GLOBAL POLITICS — BUT STILL HAS NEW POWER ECONOMICALLY.

WE WILL RETURN TO NORMALCY AT HOME... AND WITH OTHER NATIONS WILL DO DOLLAR DIPLOMACY.

PRESIDENT WARREN HARDING

IN THE 1920s, U.S. FACTORIES CRANK. INCOME FOR THE AVERAGE AMERICAN SOARS 40 PERCENT! THE NATIONAL DEBT FALLS!

BUT SOME VETERANS HAVE TROUBLE RETURNING TO AMERICAN SOCIETY.

NO MORE JIM CROW!! I AM A VETERAN!

RACE RIOTS HIT 25 CITIES IN 1919. THE KU KLUX KLAN TERRORIZES BLACK VETS TO REPRESS THEIR RIGHTS. OVER 100 BLACK PEOPLE ARE LYNCHED IN 1919.

WHITE VETERANS ALSO STRUGGLE. THE AMERICAN LEGION BEGINS IN 1919 TO GET VETS A CASH BONUS FROM CONGRESS. IT WILL TAKE YEARS TO GET IT.

IT'S LIKE AMERICANS WANT TO FORGET THERE WAS A WAR...

GERMANY CANNOT FORGET. ITS POLITICAL SYSTEM IS SHATTERED. ITS HUGE WAR DEBT LEADS TO HUGE INFLATION — AND WORTHLESS MONEY!

I'LL TRADE YOU POTATO PEELS FOR WOOD.

I'LL PAY 9 MILLION GERMAN MARKS FOR THE WOOD!

GERMANS ARE BITTER ABOUT THIS PEACE...

GERMAN POLITICIANS BETRAYED THE PEOPLE. WE WILL RISE TO GREATNESS AGAIN!!!

to be CONTINUED...